Learn to Ride!

By Charlotte Godfrey

This book belongs to:

"Riding is not a gentle hobby, to be picked up and laid down like a game of solitaire. It is a grand passion!"
-Ralph Waldo Emerson

TO THE NEW HORSEMAN:

Learn to Ride! is a guide and workbook for beginning Horsemen and horsewomen, ages 6 through 12 years.

You can write in this book:
There is a place for your name and places to make notes. There are questions throughout the book about each chapter. You can answer the questions - either with your instructor or at home by yourself. Some of the questions are about things NOT discussed in this book. These questions are asked to make you THINK and to discuss them with your instructor. So, if you can't find the answers, ask your instructor! Don't be afraid to ask. It's fun to not know something and learn the answer!

With this book and your instructor, you will learn to halter, groom, show a horse in-hand, help tack up your horse and ride a beginner dressage test (included in this book).

Welcome to the wonderful world of horses!
Have fun!

Charlotte Godfrey

TABLE OF CONTENTS: page

THE PARTS OF A HORSE

THE PARTS OF A HORSE

Now that you have a horse to ride, you need to learn the names of some of his body parts so that you can speak to other Horsemen and they will know exactly what you are talking about!

In the picture below some of the parts of the horse are labeled. Some of the parts aren't labeled. Can you find the correct names of the unlabeled parts of the horse from the list in the box?

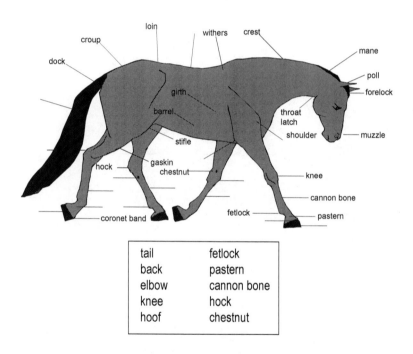

tail	fetlock
back	pastern
elbow	cannon bone
knee	hock
hoof	chestnut

If you know the names of some other parts of the horse, not listed above, List them here:

_____   _____

_____   _____

Questions about The Parts of a Horse

1. NAME 5 PARTS OF A HORSE'S LEG:

_____

_____

_____

_____

_____

2. ARE A HORSE'S EYES ON THE FRONT OF HIS FACE OR ON THE SIDE OF HIS HEAD? (Don't be fooled by the picture on this page!)

_____

_____

3. HOW DOES THE POSITION OF A HORSE'S EYES AFFECT HIS VISION: DOES HE SEE ONE PICTURE OF THE WORLD OR TWO?

_____

_____

THE COLOR OF HORSES

THE COLOR OF HORSES

Horses come in many colors. To the average person, a horse is either brown, black, white, yellowish or grey. But Horsemen and Horsewomen have special words to describe the exact color of horses. Some of the words are: bay, black, brown, dun, buckskin, chestnut, sorrel, palomino, Paint, pinto, tobiano, overo, tovero, roan, grulla, cremello, perlino, champagne, dominant white, and so on...

COMMON COLORS OF HORSES

<u>BAY HORSES</u> are light brown to dark brown or reddish in body color with black "points". Points are the mane, tail, legs and ear tips. A bay horse can also have white markings. (See the next chapter: The Markings of Horses.)

<u>BROWNS</u> can be very light brown to very dark brown in color. They have no shades of red in their hair and no black "points", but a brown horse can have white markings.

<u>CHESTNUTS/SORRELS</u> are light to dark reddish brown. The mane, tail, legs and ears are usually the same color as the horse's body. If the mane and tail are lighter in color than the body, the horse is called a "flaxen chestnut". Chestnuts might also have white markings.

<u>PINTO OR PAINT HORSES</u> have large spots of white and another color. The colors can be black, brown, chestnut, tan, yellow or grey. Pinto and Paints are different breeds. A Pinto may be any breed, but a Paint must have American Quarter Horse breeding.

<u>GREY (GRAY) HORSES</u> have black skin with white or grey hair. Grey horses are born dark and their hair turns lighter as they get older. If you own a grey horse, it will probably be a different color each year!

BLACK HORSES have pure black coats with no hair of any other color, except, possible white markings. (A black horse might look brown if the sun has bleached the hair coat.)

ROAN HORSES have a variety of coat colors with white hairs mixed in the coat color and sometimes in the mane and tail. Their legs and head are darker. They might also have white markings.

APPALOOSA COLORED HORSES have a variety of coat colors and can be roaned or "blanketed". A blanket is a large white area on a horse's rump with color spots in it. They might also have white markings.

(Appaloosa, Paint, Pinto and Palomino are also names of breed registries, as well as the names of colors.)

UNUSUAL AND RARE COLORS:

DUN HORSES have a sandy-yellow to reddish-brown hair coat. Their legs are darker than their body and may have faint "zebra" stripes on them. Dun horses always have a "dorsal" stripe - a dark stripe down the middle of their back. They might also have white markings.

BUCKSKIN HORSES are sandy-yellow or tan-colored with all black points and might also have white markings.

PALOMINO HORSES have gold or yellow coats with white or cream colored manes and tails and might also have white markings.

CHAMPAGNE colored horses look like light-colored Palominos but champagne horses have bright pink skin. Champagne foals are born with bright blue eyes, which slowly change to a hazel or greenish color as they age.

GRULLO OR GRULLA colored horses are smoky or mouse colored and usually have a dorsal stripe, shoulder striping or shadowing and some bars on the lower legs.

TRUE WHITE HORSES:

DOMINANT WHITE horses are very rare. They have pink skin, hazel or brown eyes and white hair.

SABINO WHITES have white hair, pink skin and dark eyes. Sometimes there are a few dark hairs on the poll or ears.

CREMELLOS AND PERLINOS are often mistakenly called Whites or Albinos but there are no albino horses!

(for more information on "white horses" go to: http://en.wikipedia.org/wiki/White_(horse)

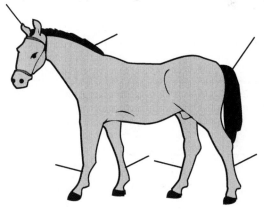

Label the "points" of the horse in the illustration above.

Questions about the Color of Horses

1. NAME 5 OF THE MOST COMMON COLORS OF HORSES.

_____

_____

_____

_____

_____

2. DESCRIBE A CHESTNUT COLORED HORSE.

_____

_____

_____

3. WHAT MAKES A ROAN HORSE ROAN?

_____

_____

4. WHEN IS A WHITE HORSE REALLY A GREY HORSE?

_____

_____

_____

THE MARKINGS OF HORSES

THE MARKINGS OF HORSES

Markings make each horse unique. Most markings are white face or leg markings with pink skin underneath them. On any horse but a grey, you can easily see white markings, but on a grey horse, you might need to wet the hair coat to find them! Other markings are non-white and "physical" markings.

COMMON WHITE MARKINGS ON THE FACE:
- a white spot on the forehead is called a "STAR"
- a ribbon of white running down the center of the face is called a "STRIPE"
- a wider area of white running down the center of the face is called a "BLAZE"
- a big white mark starting above the forehead, going to the muzzle, and extending to the side of the face is called "BALD"
- a white spot located on the muzzle, between or just below the nostrils is called a "SNIP"
(The foal pictured above can be described as having a "connected star, stripe and snip!")

COMMON WHITE MARKINGS ON THE LEGS:
- a small white band just above the hoof is called a "CORONET"
- a white marking that extends from the edge of the hoof halfway up the pastern is called a "HALF PASTERN"
- a white marking that extends from the edge of the hoof and all the way up the pastern is called a "PASTERN"
- a white marking that extends from the edge of the hoof halfway up the middle of the leg is called a "HALF STOCKING"
- a white marking that extends from edge of the hoof two-thirds of the way up the leg is called a "SOCK"
- a white marking that extends from edge of the hoof to the knee or hock is called a "STOCKING"

See if you can name the white markings on this horse.

(continued on the next page)

COMMON NON-WHITE MARKINGS:

• a dark spot on a white mark, most commonly seen just above the hoof is called an "ERMINE"

• dark spots common in chestnut or Palomino horses is called a "BEN D'OR" or "BEND-OR"spot (the name comes from the chestnut Thoroughbred horse named Ben d'Or who was known by his spots.)

• dark ears and poll on a white marked head and neck seen on Paints and Pintos is called a "MEDICINE HAT"

• a dark colored chest, with white on the shoulders, legs, belly and neck is called a "SHIELD"

a "medicine hat"

PRIMITIVE MARKINGS:

are the dorsal stripe seen in dun colored horses, shoulder stripes, leg barring, face masking, cobwebbing, mottling and guard hairs.

For an in-depth explanation of primitive markings, go to:
http://en.wikipedia.org/wiki/Primitive_markings

OTHER PHYSICAL MARKINGS:

• a "WHORL", "SWIRL" or "COWLICK" is hair growing in circles found anywhere on the body but most commonly on a horse's head. Look for your horse's facial swirl in the middle of his forehead between the eyes. Other swirls might be found on his jowl, neck, chest, belly, or in front of the stifles.

• a "GLASS EYE", "MOON EYE", "CHINA EYE", "WALL EYE" or "NIGHT EYE" is a blue colored eye. Horses with blue eyes can see as well as brown-eyed horses.

• CHESTNUTS are tough, callous-like areas on the inside of horse's legs. They are considered a mark, since each horse has unique chestnuts.

• a "PROPHET'S THUMB," is an indentation in the muscle, usually found on the horse's neck.

Questions about the Markings of Horses

1. DESCRIBE THE MARKINGS OF THE HORSE ABOVE:

_____

_____

_____

2. MATCH THE WORDS TO THE MARKINGS ON THE HORSES IN THE PICTURES BELOW:

SNIP   BLAZE   STRIPE   BALD

3. HOW CAN YOU FIND THE WHITE MARKINGS ON A VERY LIGHT COLORED GREY HORSE?

_____

HOW TO HALTER A HORSE

HOW TO HALTER A HORSE

<u>Safety tip</u>:
*Never stand
directly in front of a horse.*

1. Stand on the left side
of the horse's shoulder
about half a person's width
away from the horse or
about a hand to elbow length away.

2. Stand on the horse's left side, facing the same
direction as the horse.

3. Hold the halter out in front of the horse's face
and slip it over his nose, and up over his ears. Snap the
halter closed on the horse's left cheekbone.

NOTE: *If your halter has a
buckle fastener instead of a
snap fastener, it is a little
more complicated: After
slipping the nose piece on,
you will bring the strap on the
right side over the top of his
head and toward you to buckle
it on his left side. Have your
instructor show you how.*

Questions about Haltering a Horse

1. WHAT IS THE FIRST RULE OF SAFETY WHEN WORKING WITH HORSES?

_____

_____

_____

2. AND WHY IS THAT RULE IMPORTANT?

_____

_____

2. WHERE SHOULD YOU STAND WHEN HALTERING A HORSE?

_____

_____

3. HALTER COME IN DIFFERENT SIZES. CAN YOU NAME SOME?

_____   _____

_____   _____

HOW TO CATCH A HORSE

HOW TO CATCH A HORSE

Safety tip:
*Don't run toward, away from or chase
a horse! Walk toward the horse calmly.
He may walk or trot away from you,
he might face you and stand still or he
might walk or even trot toward you.*

Don't be afraid. Most horses want
to co-operate with humans. When
the horse is standing calmly, you can
attach the lead rope to his halter.

USING A SHANK:
The proper way to attach a lead rope with a
metal chain (also called a "shank") is:

1. Thread the snap through the left side of the horse's
halter, going inward and upward toward the horse's eye
and then drape the chain over the nosepiece of the
halter.

2. Snap the end of the shank to the bottom of the
right metal fitting of the horse's halter which is above
his mouth. If you have a long metal shank (30 inches or
more) on your lead rope, you can thread it through the
right side of the horse's halter and snap it under the
horse's chin to itself or thread the end up though the
right side of the horse's halter and snap it to the metal
ring behind the horse's eye.

NOTE: *The purpose of a shank
is to act as a "brake", similar
to the brakes on a car.
It gives you the ability
to stop your horse in
case of emergency.
Do not try to "pull"
a horse forward with
a shank. A shank's purpose
is to make a horse
stop or back up!*

Questions about Catching a Horse

1. WHAT IS THE PURPOSE OF A SHANK?

_____

_____

2. WHAT IS THE PROPER WAY TO ATTACH A SHANK
TO A HORSE'S HALTER?

_____

_____

_____

3. WHAT IS THE CORRECT WAY TO USE A SHANK?

_____

_____

4. HOW COULD A SHANK BE MISUSED?

_____

_____

HOW TO LEAD A HORSE

HOW TO LEAD
A HORSE

Which side of the horse is the handler on in this picture? The "near" or "off" side?

<u>Safety tip</u>:
Never stand directly in front of a horse. Never pull on a horse. He or she might suddenly leap forward or run backward!

1. Stand on the left side of the horse's shoulder about a person's width away from the horse.

2. Hold the lead rope by the cotton line below the metal parts. NEVER LOOP A LEAD ROPE AROUND YOUR HAND! Always hold the extra length of a lead rope (if there is any) doubled over in your left hand. This way, in case of emergency, you can open your hand and let go of the lead rope. (If you had looped the rope around your hand, it might be pulled tight by a spooked horse and you might hurt your hand or even be dragged!)

3. When you are ready to lead your horse, ask him to walk with you by giving a slight tug and release on the rope and by saying "Walk" or by clucking to him.

4. If your horse pulls back instead of going with you as you start to walk, do not pull back on him in return. Instead, relax the lead rope and say "Whoa." Then try again. Most horses will walk off without an objection. As you walk, be sure to keep away from the horse's feet by keeping a body width between you and your horse, You can use your hand, arm or elbow to keep your horse at a proper distance.

5. Turn a horse by pushing him AWAY from you. Use the lead rope and your hand on the horse's shoulder, if necessary, to push the horse away.

Questions about Leading a Horse

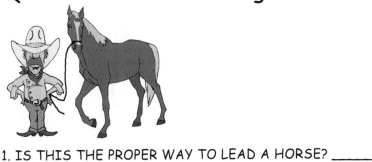

1. IS THIS THE PROPER WAY TO LEAD A HORSE? _____

2. WHY?

_____

_____

_____

_____

3. WHY IS IT IMPORTANT TO TURN A HORSE AWAY FROM YOU INSTEAD OF TOWARD YOU WHEN CHANGING DIRECTION?

_____

_____

3. WHAT IS THE PROPER WAY TO MAKE A HORSE BACK UP ON THE LEAD LINE?

_____

_____

HOW TO GROOM A HORSE

HOW TO GROOM A HORSE

(Written with a lot of help from Zoe Krause)

<u>Safety tip</u>:
*Never stand directly in front
of or behind a horse.*

What's wrong in this picture?

Grooming is a very important part of
caring for your horse. It is a good idea
to groom your horse every day, even
if you don't plan to ride him or her.
Grooming can create a bond
between you and your horse. It's also
a good way to check your horse closely for cuts,
scratches, skin irritations, hoof problems or anything out
of the ordinary.

1. Groom your horse in cross ties. Do not try to groom a
horse in a stall and do not try to groom a loose horse.

2. Stand on the horse's side. Start with your horse's
head, and don't forget: "NEVER STAND DIRECTLY IN
FRONT OF OR BEHIND A HORSE."
Use the rubber mitt to rub loose hairs from your
horse's face, then brush the loose hairs off with the
softest brush in your grooming kit. (Grooming brushes
come in a variety of textures from soft to stiff.)

3. Next, use the rubber curry in circular motions all
over your horse's body, starting behind the head.
Rubber currys are great for getting loose hair and
dirt off the horse. Rub in circular motions over your
horse's body, and use lots of "elbow grease" when you
curry! But don't use the rubber curry on the legs.

Why do you think the rubber curry shouldn't be used on
a horse's legs?

(continued on page 41)

Some of the tools used to Groom a Horse

DIFFERENT KINDS OF BRUSHES:

Hard, soft and in-between

RUBBER CURRY:
removes dirt, dried mud, etc.

RUBBER MITT: use on face and legs

MANE AND TAIL COMBS AND BRUSHES:

When you rub your horse with the rubber curry, you may find that Your horse has a favorite "itchy" spot!
Did you find more than one itchy spot? Write what itchy spot or spots your horse has:

_____

_____

4. Most grooming kits have at least 2 brushes: a soft brush and a stiffer one. After currying, use the stiff brush in short, quick strokes in the direction that your horse's hair grows. A horse's hair usually grows from head to tail, but there are exceptions, called "swirls". (See page 22.)

How many swirls you can find on your horse's body?

on my horse's head:	_____	(number)
on my horse's neck:	_____	(number)
on my horse's barrel:	_____	(number)
on my horse's legs:	_____	(number)

The soft brush is used next. Use the soft brush the same way you used the stiff brush: short, quick strokes all over your horse's body. The soft brush is the last brush you use and that is why it is sometimes called the "finishing" brush.

5. Groom your horse's legs first with the rubber mitt to rub dirt and hair loose. After that, use the finishing brush.

6. The hoof pick is used to clean out a horse's hooves. Sometimes a horse will get a stone wedged in its hoof and can't get it out without your help. Sometimes the hoof is full of dirt, or even manure. Dirt and manure can lead to a diseased hoof and lameness, so using the hoof pick is important!

More tools used to Groom a Horse

SHAMPOO AND SPONGES

DE-TANGLE SPRAY

HOOF CARE:
hoof pick, hoof oil and brush

OOPS!

To use the hoof pick, stand on the side of your horse, facing his or her tail. Your instructor will show you how to lift each foot and clean out the hoof. If your hoof pick has a brush on it, use the brush to finish cleaning out the hoof.

7. Forelocks, manes and tails can be groomed with brushes or combs. Start at the bottom and work your way up, being careful not to tear the hair. If you find a knot or a tangle, slowly work it out with your fingers or with a brush. De-tangling sprays can help. Never use scissors, a knife or a hoof pick to get tangles out of a horse's hair! Ask your instructor if you need help.

Horses grow long hair in other places on their bodies, besides their forelock, mane and tail. Can you find other places on your horse's body where the hair grows long?

See if you can find the answers to the following questions:

1. Do horses have feathers?

_____

2. What is a bridle path?

_____

3. What facial hair is usually clipped for show grooming?

_____

_____

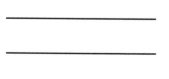

_____

(You can find the answers to these questions in books on grooming, on the internet or by asking your instructor.)

Questions about Grooming a Horse

1. WHAT GROOMING TOOL IS BEST
FOR GETTING DRIED MUD OFF A HORSE?

_____

_____

_____

2. HOW SHOULD YOU BRUSH A HORSE'S TAIL ?

_____

_____

_____

3. WHAT DO YOU CLEAN A HORSE'S FEET WITH?

_____

4. WHY IS IT A GOOD IDEA TO
GROOM YOUR HORSE BEFORE RIDING?

_____

_____

_____

_____

HOW TO SHOW A HORSE AT HALTER OR IN HAND

HOW TO SHOW A HORSE AT HALTER OR IN HAND

<u>Safety tip</u>:
Keep yourself and your horse a safe distance away from other horses. Stay out of the "kicking zone".

1. Stand on the left side of the horse with your toes pointed toward the horse's front feet.

2. Always move the horse <u>away</u> from you, never toward you.

3. Present the horse to the judge so that he or she always sees the whole body of the horse. That means that you will have to move as the judge walks around your horse to inspect him. The horse must stand still. Your instructor will show you how to move so the judge can see your horse.

4. Hold the lead line (used for Western classes) or bridle rein (used for English classes) in the right and left hand. In English classes, in which horses are shown in a bridle, the reins are looped and folded in your left hand and the right hand holds the reins coming directly from the bit. In Western classes, the halter's lead line is held in the right hand well away from the horse's head and the end of the lead line is held in the left hand.

5. Listen carefully to the judge or the ring steward when they tell you what to do. They will tell you to walk or trot the horse or both and where to do it. Listen carefully and present your horse proudly!

Have fun!

Questions about Showing a Horse At Halter or In Hand

1. WHAT STYLE IS PICTURED HERE: ENGLISH OR WESTERN?

_____

2. HOW CAN YOU TELL?

_____

_____

1. WHAT STYLE IS PICTURED HERE: ENGLISH OR WESTERN?

_____

2. HOW CAN YOU TELL?

_____

_____

_____

5. IS THE RIDER IN THE SECOND PICTURE HOLDING HER HORSE PROPERLY TO SHOW IN AN IN HAND CLASS?

_____

_____

ABOUT RIDING

ABOUT RIDING

Most horses have 4 "gaits". ("Gaits" can be thought of as the way a horse moves its legs according to how fast it is going.) However, some horses, usually called "gaited", have different gaits! For instance, the Icelandic breed has a gait called the "tolt" and Walking Horses "rack". But, for our discussion of gaits, we will stick to the 4 gaits common to most horses: the walk, the trot or jog, the canter or lope and the gallop.

1. WALK

The WALK is a "4 beat" gait, meaning that the horse   moves one leg at the time: one, two, three, four. You can hear four separate footfalls.

* Listen to the horse's footfalls and count out loud as your horse walks: "One, two, three, four!"
* See if you can <u>feel</u> which leg is making the sound you hear!

2. TROT (English) or JOG (Western)

The English TROT is a bouncy, "2-beat" gait in which the horse moves two legs at the same time and both hit the ground at about the same time. The same is true for the Western JOG, except that it is slower, and it is not as bouncy as the English TROT.

* Watch a horse TROT or JOG and see which legs are moving together!
* Count out loud as your horse trots: "One, two, one two, one, two!"
* See if you can feel which shoulder is moving forward when you count "One, two!" Don't look down to check until you say out loud which shoulder is moving forward!

3. <u>CANTER</u> (English) or <u>LOPE</u> (Western)
The CANTER is a 3-beat gait. The horse pushes off with a hind leg, lands on 2 legs (a front and a hind) and then on a front leg.
The canter is a "rolling" gait and it will make your hips roll forward and back as if you were dancing! It may be scarey at first, but you will enjoy the canter when you get used to the new feeling!

4. <u>GALLOP</u>
The GALLOP is a fast 4-beat gait. The horse springs off one hindleg, then the other, then lands on one foreleg and then the other.
The gallop can be seen at gaming shows, in horse racing and on TV when the good guys are chasing the bad guys! (The "Hand Gallop" seen at Hunter Shows is actually a three-beat canter.)

DID YOU KNOW:
The average horse can gallop 25-30 miles per hour! Thoroughbred horses are known for their races, however, the fastest galloping horse is the American Quarter horse! According to reports, the fastest American Quarter Horses can gallop up to 55 miles per hour!

To see a moving horse in all four gaits on the web, go to:
http://www.horseclub.co.uk/paces.htm
For an in-depth explanations of horse's gaits go to:
http://en.wikipedia.org/wiki/Horse_gait

Questions about Riding

1. NAME FOUR GAITS OF THE HORSE.

_____

_____

_____

_____

2. NAME 2 FOUR-BEAT GAITS.

_____

_____

3. HOW DOES THE TROT AND CANTER DIFFER FROM THE JOG AND LOPE?

_____

_____

_____

NOTES:

_____

_____

RIDE SAFELY

RIDE SAFELY

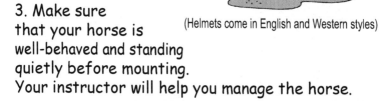

1. Always wear
a helmet!

2. Stand on the
left side of the horse.

3. Make sure
that your horse is
well-behaved and standing
quietly before mounting.
Your instructor will help you manage the horse.

(Helmets come in English and Western styles)

4. Make your horse stand still after you mount and
get settled in the saddle. Ask for help if needed.

5. Sit in the saddle as if you are standing on the
ground, except that your knees are bent. In other
words, if the horse were taken out from under you,
you should be able to keep your knees bent and not
fall on your face or your fanny! So lower your heels
and sit up straight!

Don't be afraid to ask lots of questions.

Tell your instructor if you are afraid.

Everyone falls off a horse eventually. If you fall
off your horse, leave the dust on your clothes and
get right back on!

Have fun!

Questions about Riding Safely

1. WHAT PIECE OF RIDING EQUIPMENT IS MISSING IN THIS PICTURE?

_____

2. WHAT IS THE RIDER DOING CORRECTLY?

_____

_____

_____

3. HOW COULD THE RIDER IMPROVE THE WAY HE IS SITTING IN THE SADDLE?

_____

_____

_____

4 WHY IS IT IMPORTANT TO SIT UP STRAIGHT IN THE SADDLE?

_____

_____

More Questions about Riding Safely

5. WHY SHOULD YOU RIDE WITH YOUR HEELS DOWN?

_____

_____

_____

6. WHY IS IT IMPORTANT FOR YOUR HORSE TO STAND STILL AFTER YOU ARE MOUNTED?

_____

_____

_____

NOTES:

_____

_____

_____

_____

_____

_____

More Questions about Riding Safely

7. DID THESE 2 RIDERS PASS EACH OTHER CORRECTLY?

_____

_____

_____

8. WHAT WOULD YOU CHANGE ABOUT THE WAY
THEY ARE SITTING ON THEIR HORSES?

_____

_____

_____

9. WHAT WOULD YOU CHANGE ABOUT THEIR RIDING
ATTIRE?

_____

_____

ARENA SAFETY

ARENA SAFETY

Ride with people who are careful and know how to be safe. Some of the generally accepted rules of arena safety are:

1. Slow horses (Horses going in a slower gait than others) stay to the inside.

2. Faster horses (Horses going at a faster gait than others) get the rail.

3. Pass horses left shoulder to left shoulder. Ask your instructor what left shoulder to left shoulder looks like!

4. If you must change direction, tell every one where you are going: "Outside...Inside...To the rail...On your right...The second jump...To the out-gate..." etc.

5. If a horse gets loose, is misbehaving or if some- one is jumping, you will hear: "HEADS UP!" That is your signal to watch what is going on in the area. You may have to stop your horse and get off. Whenever you ride, listen, watch and be careful!

Your instructor will help you start riding in a safe environment.

Listen, watch, be careful...and ask questions!

Have fun!

Questions about Arena Safety

1. NAME THREE OF THE ARENA RULES OF SAFETY.

_____

_____

_____

2. WHAT SHOULD YOU SHOUT OUT TO ALERT
EVERYONE IF THERE IS A LOOSE HORSE, SOMEONE
JUMPING OR TROUBLE IN THE ARENA?

_____

NOTES:

_____

_____

_____

_____

_____

_____

_____

_____

About Feeding Horses

About Feeding Horses

Safety tip:
Always feed horses through a fence or in the feeder in their stall. When feeding a stalled horse, stay outside the stall and feed them through the feeder opening with an adult's supervision. And, remember: watch your fingers!

Horses are grazing animals. The have a small stomach and are supposed to eat small amounts of food all day.

Stabled horse may have pastures, but they work for a living and cannot stay in their pastures and eat all day. They are fed hay and "concentrates" to make up for the time that they would have otherwise spent in their pastures grazing.

Concentrates are grains, sweet feed (grains mixed with molasses) or pellets. Most stabled horses will eat 10-15 pounds of hay and 2 - 7 pounds of concentrates each day. The exact amount of hay and concentrates fed depends upon their work level, size and a horse's "metabolism." ("Metabolism" can be thought of as the way a body uses food.)

Nervous and hard-working horses need more feed than calm, lazy or under-exercised horses. Older horses may need more feed than other horses because their teeth might be missing or they are unable to absorb nutrients as well as younger horses.

Horses can eat some human foods. They enjoy fruits, grains and donuts! However, chocolate is not good for horses, so no chocolate donuts, please!

Questions about Feeding Horses

What does a horse eat when it grazes?

Grass?	____ Yes	____ No
Flowers?	____ Yes	____ No
Bark from trees?	____ Yes	____ No
Dirt?	____ Yes	____ No

Can you name other things a horse might eat when it grazes?

_____

_____

_____

Why would a horse eat tree bark?

_____

_____

Would a horse eat wood fences?   ____ Yes ____ No

Why would a horse lick clay soil?

_____

_____

_____

How much water does a horse drink each day?

_____

HOW TO FEED TREATS
TO A HORSE SAFELY

HOW TO FEED TREATS TO A HORSE SAFELY:

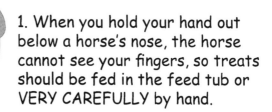

1. When you hold your hand out below a horse's nose, the horse cannot see your fingers, so treats should be fed in the feed tub or VERY CAREFULLY by hand.

2. If you feed a treat by hand, you must be careful not to curl your fingers upward around the treat. Place the treat on the palm of your hand and hold your fingers flat, offering the treat in the middle of your palm.

3. Do not feed too many treats to horses and spoil them. Some horses get very pushy and demand treats, so it is really best to feed treats in the feed tub and not too often.

4. Horses enjoy carrots, apples, grapes, dates and commercially made treats. What other fruits and veggies do you think a horse might enjoy?

_____

_____

_____

_____

HORSE TREAT RECIPES

You can make these at home!

CARROT & OATMEAL COOKIES

1 cup of oatmeal
1 cup of flour
1 cup of chopped carrots
1 teaspoon of salt
1 teaspoon of sugar
2 teaspoons of corn oil
1/4 cup of molasses

Mix ingredients and shape into cookies.
Bake on a non-stick cookie sheet
for 20-30 minutes at 325 degrees until done.
Cool in refrigerator before feeding!

SWEET APPLE & BRAN COOKIES

1 cup of sweet feed
2 - 3 cups of bran
1 cup of ground, stabilized flax seed
1 tablespoon of salt
4 large chopped apples
1 cup of molasses
1/2 cup of brown sugar
1 cup of applesauce

Mix ingredients and shape into cookies,
adding more bran to thicken, if needed.
Bake on a non-stick cookie sheet
for about 20-30 minutes at 300 degrees.
Turn the cookies over and bake until done.
Cool before feeding.

PEPPERMINT TREATS

2 cups of flour
1 cup of oats
1/4 cup of molasses
10 crushed peppermints
2 large apples, chopped

Mix flour and oats together. Add molasses.
Add water slowly until mixture is doughy.
Add peppermints and apples. Cook at 350 degrees
in a greased or non-stick pan until golden brown.
Chill before serving!

BREAKFAST TREAT MIX

1 apple cut into small pieces
1 cup of cracked corn
1 cup of pelleted horse feed
1 cup of uncooked oatmeal
1/2 teaspoon salt
1 cup of breakfast cereal (Remember:
no chocolate!)
syrup, honey, or molasses
powdered sugar to sprinkle on top

Mix corn, oatmeal, apple, grain, cereal, pellets and salt.
Drizzle on syrup and sprinkle with powdered sugar.
Chill in refrigerator over night.

TASTY HORSE TACOS

Tortillas
1 cup of molasses
2 cups of sliced carrots
2 cups of sliced apples
2 cups of grapes
3 cups of sweet feed

Mix sweet feed and molasses.
Mix in the sliced carrots, apples, and grapes.
Wrap the mixture in tortillas,
Chill in refrigerator over night and serve.

Question about Feeding Treats Safely

1. IS THIS A SAFE WAY TO FEED A TREAT?

_____

2. WHY?

_____

_____

_____

3. WHAT WOULD BE A BETTER WAY TO FEED CARROTS TO HORSES?

_____

_____

_____

3. WHAT ARE SOME HEALTHY THINGS TO FEED AS TREATS TO HORSES?

_____

_____

_____

ABOUT DRESSAGE

ABOUT DRESSAGE

"Dressage" is a French word that means to "dress" or train.

The great thing about dressage is that it teaches you and the horse to communicate without words. It teaches you how to use your legs, your position, your weight and your hands to tell the horse what you want. It teaches your horse to be obedient and to pay attention to your commands.

Dressage is ridden with a snaffle bit and can be ridden in any saddle for training purposes. Formal dressage shows require an English saddle for English Dressage or a Western saddle for Western Dressage competition.

Dressage teaches you and your horse to become true partners and is a good foundation for any riding discipline: Jumping, Western Pleasure, Reining, Gymkhana etc.

Dressage shows consist of tests ridden at different levels of difficulty: Introduction tests are for beginning dressage riders and green horses who want to show walk and trot. Training Level tests are for those who canter and are new to dressage. First Level tests are for horses who are learning leg yields and lengthenings in the trot and canter. Second Level tests are for horses beginning collection. After Second Level, there is Third and Forth Levels, Prix St. Georges, Intermediare I and II and Grand Prix, which is the level of dressage you see at the Olympics!

Riding a dressage test will show how much you and the horse have learned together!

Have fun!

BEGINNER DRESSAGE TEST
(English or Western)

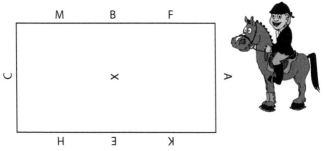

Enter at A in trot or jog
Halt at X through the walk
Salute and proceed toward C at the walk

At C, turn right
At M, trot or jog and proceed to B
At B, circle right 20 meters*

Returning to B, go straight ahead
Between B and F, walk

Between A and K, trot or jog,
Then, K, X, M trot across the diagonal

Between M and C, walk

Between H and E, trot or jog,
And at E, circle left 20 meters
Then go straight ahead

Between K and A, walk
Proceed to A

At A, go down the center line
At X, halt and salute
(leave the arena at a walk)

Your instructor will show you the 20 meter circle.

Notes:

_____

_____

_____

_____

_____

_____

_____

_____

_____

_____

_____

_____

Notes:

Notes:

Notes:

_____

_____

_____

_____

_____

_____

_____

_____

_____

_____

_____

Notes:

_____

_____

_____

_____

_____

_____

_____

_____

_____

_____

_____

_____

Notes:

Notes:

_____

_____

_____

_____

_____

_____

_____

_____

_____

_____

_____

_____

Notes:

Notes:

Congratulations to you for completing
Learn to Ride!

There will be many horses in your life. Some
will be very special. One or two may change
your life. From now on, wherever you go
and whatever you do, you can call yourself a
HORSEMAN or a HORSEWOMAN!

Charlotte Godfrey

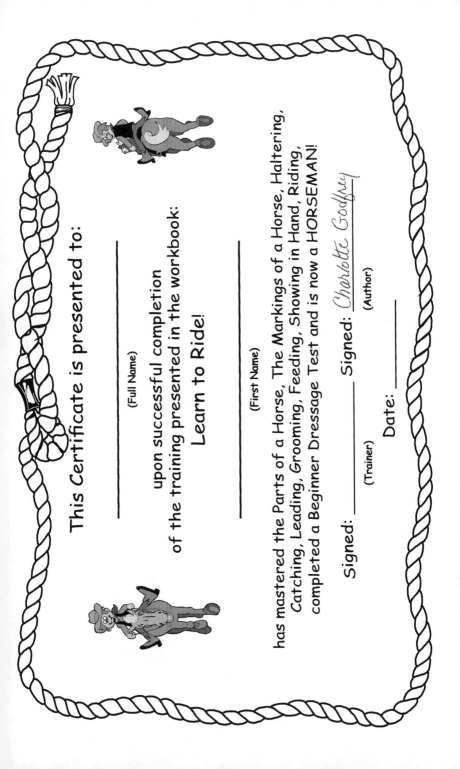

This Certificate is presented to:

_____
(Full Name)

upon successful completion
of the training presented in the workbook:
Learn to Ride!

_____
(First Name)

has mastered the Parts of a Horse, The Markings of a Horse, Haltering,
Catching, Leading, Grooming, Feeding, Showing in Hand, Riding,
completed a Beginner Dressage Test and is now a HORSEMAN!

Signed: _____   Signed: _Charlotte Godfrey_
          (Trainer)   (Author)

Date: _____

About the Author:

Charlotte Godfrey's first riding experience was with her Grandfather's working mule, Maggie, who she jumped bareback - until Grandpa found Charlotte lying flat on the ground after jumping an obstacle under her Grandmother's wire clothesline. When he discovered that she wasn't decapitated, he forbade her to jump and bought her a horse who tried to kill her in other ways.

That horse, who she dubbed "Little Boy", was a sturdy grey gelding who knew several ways of getting rid of children. After bucking her off, biting and dragging her by the stomach, he tried to run her down in the pasture one day when she went to catch him. Not willing to give up, she was forced to learn the importance of being the "leader" (or Boss Mare). Once he respected her, Little Boy taught her how to ride and survive. She experienced her first collected canter riding him and has loved dressage ever since.

Charlotte and her partner, Michael Sexton, own Goodells Equestrian Center in Goodells, Michigan. She is still trying to master the art of dressage... "I'm gonna write a book about my experience with dressage," she says. "It'll be called Twenty years at Training Level!"

photo by Mike Sexton

The author is pictured above with Kajun ("Big Guy") and Gotsno ("Tough Guy").

www.goodellsequestriancenter.com
facebook: Charlotte Godfrey
Goodells Equestrian Center

THANKS...

To Jeralyn Glod for being the best kid editor I ever
met and to Zoe Krause, instructor extraordinaire,
for her help with the grooming chapter and for being
the final word on the value of this little book.

Charlotte